By Ymkje Wideman-van der Laan
Illustrated by Rob Feldman

Copyright © 2012 Ymkje Wideman-van der Laan
All rights reserved. Designed by Awexdesign
ISBN-10: 1475102712
ISBN-13: 978-1475102710

For Logan, who one day asked, "Autism is…?"

While talking to her friend one day,
I heard my grandma talk and say
That I was just the greatest lad,
And that it's autism that I had.

She talked some more and again I heard
Her use that mysterious autism word.
Now what, I wondered, could this be,
My grandma said was part of me.

I pulled her sleeve and she bent down,
And asked me why I wore a frown.
She knew that something was amiss
When I shouted, "Autism is...?"

She smiled and told me not to worry,
Or get into a great big flurry.
That night before I'd go to bed,
She would explain.

                 Here's what she said...

You have a very special brain
That can move faster than a train.

It tells your body to move about,

So you will spin,

and jump,

and shout.

'Cause moving fast is so much fun,
And off you go for another run.

Your brain sends signals to your ear,
So the tiniest little sounds you hear.

Your eyes see more than I can see,
And never miss an ant or bee.

Your brain just loves to learn to read,
And remembers words like centipede.

It wants to learn and understand,
So you explore things without end.

Sometimes you get a little tired,
Because your brain has been so wired...

...from all you see, and hear, and do,
And all the running and jumping, too.

You might start spinning,

lie on the ground,

Or make a great big yelling sound.

That's how it is you let me know
You need a calm, safe place to go.

Your brain works in a different way
From friends' at school, but that's okay.

All kids are different, that's a fact,
And this is just the way YOU act.

So now you know, nothing's amiss,
Because that's just what autism is!

Logan drew 10 little bees and hid them in the pages of this book. Can you find them?

About the Author

Ymkje Wideman-van der Laan is a writer, editor, and proofreader. In 2006, she assumed the care of her 6-month old grandson, Logan. There were signs of autism at an early age, and the diagnosis became official in 2009. She has been his advocate, and passionate about promoting autism awareness ever since. Logan is the inspiration behind *Autism Is...?* and other children's books she wrote for him. You can find out more about her and her books at www.ymkje.com and www.autism-is.com.

Note to Parents and Caregivers

Autism Spectrum Disorder (ASD) is a disability that affects an estimated 1 out of 68 children (1 in 42 boys and 1 in 189 girls) in the US alone. It is a "spectrum" disorder because its impact on development can range from mild to severe. The areas of development most affected are social interaction and communication skills, difficulties with verbal and non-verbal communication, and leisure play.

Someone wisely said, "If you have met one person with autism, you have met one person with autism." The characteristics are different with each unique individual, and so are the ways to interact, teach, and care for them.

You may or may not wish to explain autism to your child at a young age, but if you do, I hope this book can help make it easier for you, as it did for me when explaining autism to Logan. His inquisitive mind wanted to know, and once he read this story, even before it was illustrated, he was satisfied with the answer.

The Author

Made in United States
Orlando, FL
14 December 2023

40463152R00015